CREATIVE ABUNDANCE

CREATIVE ABUNDANCE

Keys to Spiritual and Material Prosperity

ELIZABETH CLARE PROPHET

MARK L. PROPHET

SUMMIT UNIVERSITY PRESS®

CREATIVE ABUNDANCE
Keys to Spiritual and Material Prosperity
by Elizabeth Clare Prophet and Mark L. Prophet
Copyright © 1998 by Summit University Press
All rights reserved

Library of Congress Control Number: 2001095004
ISBN 0-922729-38-7

Summit University 🐚 Press®

06   05   04   03   02   01   9   8   7   6   5   4

CONTENTS

$\mathcal{A}$bundance is more than money. Abundance is the flow of energy that comes to us from the universal source of life as both spiritual and material prosperity. Abundance is love and wisdom, talents and virtues, money and material goods—whatever we need to fulfill our life's purpose.

Energy should be flowing freely to us and through us to materialize abundance. If we are not experiencing that flow of abundance, we have to ask ourselves why.

What is it within us or around us that is blocking prosperity?

What is blocking the flow of God's energy to us?

Creative Abundance

This book can help you answer these questions. It contains keys for magnetizing the spiritual and material abundance you need. These keys are drawn from the profound writings of the master Saint Germain and from teachings my late husband, Mark, and I have given over the last forty years.

Saint Germain, who is an expert in the spiritual and physical transformation known as alchemy, writes:

"How long will you spend your energy struggling to eke out a bare existence from nature's cupboard, which to some seems bare indeed, when all your needs can be met by mastering the cosmic laws that Jesus and other great teachers have demonstrated by their own lives?...

"With you—as with God—all things are possible."

The possibilities for creative abundance are endless. I encourage you to explore them as you practice the simple techniques that follow to create your personal alchemy of abundance. And please send me your success stories—I would love to hear about your victories!

Elizabeth Clare Prophet

Note: Because gender-neutral language can at times be cumbersome and confusing, we have used the pronouns *he* and *him* to refer to God or to the individual and *man* or *mankind* to refer to people in general. We have used these terms simply for readability and consistency. They are not intended to exclude women or the feminine aspect of God, for God is both masculine and feminine.

BE GRATEFUL FOR EVERYTHING THAT HAPPENS TO YOU

If the only prayer you say in your whole life is "thank you," that would suffice.   —Meister Eckhart

There is an inherent law of mind that we increase whatever we praise. The whole of creation responds to praise and is glad.   —Charles Fillmore

Praise God for the joy and beauty of his creation—not the least of which is the beauty of your own soul. Continually thank God for what you are and what you have, and you will see how your abundance will increase.

———— ∞ ————

Affirmations:

Let God be magnified! (Ps. 70:4)

∞

Let ~~the LORD~~ God be magnified, which hath pleasure in the prosperity of ~~his~~ Me ~~servant~~! (Ps. 35:27)

———— ∞ ————

Be grateful to God for everything that happens to you. Everything—the negatives, the positives, the karma, the calamities—because they are teachers, they are lessons. And if things aren't going right, praise God for letting them go wrong to remind you that there is some adjustment you have to make in order to get on with your spiritual progress.

We are all on a path of initiation. Earth is a schoolroom, and we are intended to graduate from that schoolroom. The lessons we learn along life's way are what propel us from one grade to the next.

Yet isn't it true that we have all faced situations in life where we couldn't see a single reason why we should praise God? It is important to realize that anything coming at you—whether it's Mars or a Mack truck, whether it's your mother-in-law or your manager—is energy coming your way. Bless the messenger who delivers that bundle of energy and then take the energy out of the seemingly negative matrix. Reclaim it and transmute it into something positive.

Don't wait until you have your full and final victory over life's challenges to be happy, to rejoice, to give praise and blessings to life. Praising God and being grateful every day is a key to the victory of your soul.

———— ∞ ————

AFFIRMATIONS:

God
~~LORD~~, I do give thee thanks for the abundance that is mine.

In the name I AM THAT I AM, I AM expanding this day all that I have that is of God—through love, through praise, through thanksgiving!

———— ∞ ————

Be Grateful for Everything

Praise God in everyone you meet. Try and give everyone you meet a positive spin. Give yourself the assignment to find something wonderful about every person you meet—then tell it to them. That something may be just what they need to lift them out of the doldrums or to dispel the sense that there is nothing really special about them. There *is* something special about everyone, and you can help them see what it is.

"This day, O God, I will give a positive spin to everyone you send me." When you tell that to God, you're going to have the world beating a path to your doorway, because there are so many people who need that positive spin.

FORGIVE YOURSELF

*Self-forgiveness is a great birth.
... It is the state of being that arises
from our willingness to accept, without judgment, all of who we are, our
seeming shortcomings as well as
our innate glory.* —Robin Casarjian

$\mathcal{I}$ have met people now and then who say, "I just can't forgive myself for this terrible thing I did." They'll even say, "I know God has forgiven me. But I just can't forgive myself."

If you feel you have done something unforgivable or you have misused an-other's funds or spent funds unwisely, please don't hesitate to turn to God for forgiveness and be willing to set things right.

When we cannot ask for forgiveness or receive it, in reality that means we are too proud to accept a gift from God. We want to do it all on our own. But, in fact, we all need God.

Perhaps you acted selfishly or out of a desire for material things that you didn't really need. It doesn't matter. Don't walk around with a sense of guilt, thinking "I am in debt. Woe is me because I have bought these things that I don't need. I've invested unwisely. I've wasted the money God gave me. Now look at the mess I've made of my life."

Whatever mess you may have made

of your finances, accept God's forgiveness, affirm the worthiness of God, and affirm yourself as the mirror image of God.

AFFIRMATION:

In the name of my I AM Presence, I claim the worthiness of God and myself as the mirror image of God!

Remember, you are made in the image and likeness of God. Your soul is meant to be a giant mirror of God. Keep the mirror polished. Look in the mirror and see God's face smiling at you—and return that smile.

Every time something threatens to cloud the mirror—you feel a sense of injustice, you become annoyed, something unexpectedly pops up out of your unconscious—keep on polishing the mirror so you can be a more perfect reflection of God.

Speak to any force, within or without, that nags at you and tries to put you down and say:

"My God has forgiven me. I accept that forgiveness and I forgive myself. I am so grateful God has given me another opportunity that I will forgive all wrongs that anyone has ever done to me or will ever do to me!"

AFFIRMATION:

I AM forgiveness acting here,
Casting out all doubt and fear,
Setting ~~men~~ _{All} forever free
With wings of cosmic victory.

I AM calling in full power
For forgiveness every hour;
To all life in every place
I flood forth forgiving grace.

(repeat three times
or in multiples of three)

ABANDON ANXIETY

I ASK God to Let ME

*Fear less, hope more; eat less,
chew more; whine less, breathe more;
talk less, say more; hate less, love
more;* /and *all good things are yours.*
Stop
—Swedish proverb

I ASK God to Let my
and
Anxiety ~~must~~ *go.* ~~It must be~~
*replaced by faith and solemn confi-
dence in the outworking of the divine
plan.* —Saint Germain

$\mathcal{S}$aint Germain tells us that anxiety is
a major deterrent to precipitating, or
bringing into the physical, what we need.
We cannot be a clear channel for the
flow of spiritual and material abundance

into our life until we abandon anxiety.

I firmly believe that if God has it, we can get it! For as Jesus said: "Fear not, little flock; for it is the Father's good pleasure to give you the kingdom." When we entertain doubt or fear, we cannot receive the kingdom of God (i.e., the consciousness of God) or his abundance.

Saint Germain says it is a fallacy to think that the future will bring us something that is not available to us today. "Life is abundant—here, now and forever," he says. "Wherever you are, it needs only to be tapped."

In the writings of the masters recorded by Helena Roerich, we learn that "of all the destructive energies, one should mark the vibration of fear, because fear can destroy each creative vibration.... The manifestation of fear is a barrier against each undertaking."

How many creative vibrations do you have daily? You have billions, because every drop of energy that descends to you from God is a creative vibration. These are endless currents of light that make up the stream of universal consciousness. These are the potential to create.

Fear destroys innumerable possibilities, for when we have fear anywhere in our world we negate the power of the creative vibrations flowing to us.

Instead of letting these vibrations move freely through us and arrange themselves in the positive patterns God has designed for us, anxiety causes this energy to take on the patterns of our fears and worries. And as we learn from Job, "The thing which I greatly feared is come upon me, and that which I was afraid of is come unto me."

When you think about it, anxiety is really doubt that our Creator can supply us with what we need. Yet we know that God has an unlimited source of energy, and that we have access to that energy.

The Taoist master Chuang Tzu taught: "The sagelike man knows the way of what the ancients called the Heavenly Treasure House. He may pour into it without its being filled; he may pour from it without its being exhausted."

Have you ever seen a master who was a worrywart? The great masters of East and West have discovered this great key to creative abundance: sometimes we just have to get out of the way so that God can walk through the door. "God expects but one thing of you," said the Christian mystic Meister Eckhart, "and that is that you should come out of yourself... and let God be God in you."

You can use simple affirmations to help free yourself from the doubt and fear that blocks your creative abundance. As you give these affirmations, visualize in your outstretched hands whatever you are asking God to supply you with—whether it's a new job, wisdom or the money you need to go to college.

In your mind's eye, see violet and green spiritual flames springing up all around you. The violet flame, a high-frequency spiritual energy, is the flame of transmutation that can dissolve the causes behind our fears.[1] The green flame is the flame of abundance.

You can also visualize a brilliant white flame tinged with green, known as the fearlessness flame. See it penetrating all feelings of doubt and fear, gloom and doom. As you recite the following affirmations, see the phantoms of fear and doubt leaving your aura as the flames leap up all around you.

Abandon Anxiety

———— ∞ ————

AFFIRMATIONS:

I AM a being of violet fire!
I AM the purity God desires!

∞

I AM free from fear and doubt,
Casting want and misery out,
Knowing now all good supply
Ever comes from realms on high.

I AM the hand of God's own
    fortune
Flooding forth the treasures
    of light,
Now receiving full abundance
To supply each need of life.

> (repeat three times
> or in multiples of three)

———— ∞ ————

FIRE UP YOUR FAITH

Fear knocked at the door. Faith answered. No one was there.
—Inscription over the mantle of Hinds' Head Hotel, England

Faith antidotes fear. Faith is the matrix, the pattern, of those things that we will bring into manifestation. That's why faith is so important; if we lose our faith or our vision, the foundation of our creative endeavor will crumble.

Have faith that whatever you place before God as part of your personal alchemy for abundance will be refined until it is perfected. Wait for it.

For many, waiting for the fulfillment

of the promise is their greatest test. And often, they become discouraged and give up just before God is about to answer their prayers.

The apostle James tells us that patience and faith go hand in hand. He writes:

> Let patience have her perfect work, that ye may be perfect and entire, wanting nothing.
>
> If any of you lack wisdom, let him ask of God, that giveth to all men liberally and upbraideth not; and it shall be given him.

In other words, if we are patient, we will be "entire"—full, whole, having no wants. God gives to us liberally and does not scold us for asking for the bountiful gifts of his love. But ask wisely and well, for the gifts and riches of the spirit are the gifts we should seek above all. James continues:

> But let him ask in faith, nothing wavering. For he that wavereth is like a wave of the sea driven with the wind and tossed.
>
> For let not that man think that he shall receive any thing of the Lord.
>
> A double minded man is unstable in all his ways.

Do you have faith one moment and doubt the next? This is wavering. Wavering can shatter the matrix of your plans every time. Here are some affirmations you can use in those moments of doubt to fire up your faith that God will supply your every need.

———— ∞ ————

AFFIRMATIONS:

Preserve me, O God: for in thee do I put my trust!   (Ps. 16:1)

∞

O God, you are my infinite and abundant supply!

∞

O dearest Michael, Archangel of Faith,
Around my life protection seal;
Let each new day my faith increase
That God in life is all that's real.

———— ∞ ————

Years ago, Mark Prophet gave a formula for abundance, which he taught us to repeat three times a day for five minutes without interruption: Recite "I AM! I AM! I AM! the resurrection and the life of my finances!" three times followed by "now made manifest in my hands and use today!"

"As you recite this affirmation," he said, "visualize in your hands the desired abundance or the amount of money you need. Keep up this exercise with full faith in the light of God that never fails until you get results.

"Be certain that you submit your request to the will of God, that your motive is only to serve and bless all life, and that you are also willing to go to work to do your part to precipitate your own supply."

————— ∞ —————

ᴀꜰꜰɪʀᴍᴀᴛɪᴏɴꜱ:

useFul to this Earth everyDay MY God-MY HusBonG

I AM! I AM! I AM! the resurrection and the life of my finances!

(give three times)

Now made manifest in my hands
and use today!

∞

I AM! I AM! I AM! the resurrection and the life of my finances and the
U.S. economy! (give three times)

Now made manifest in my hands
and use today!

————— ∞ —————

VISUALIZE

Attention is the key; for where
man's attention goes, there goes
his energy, and he himself can only
follow. —Saint Germain

$\mathcal{W}$e should always begin our experiments in abundance by creating and then repeatedly visualizing a blueprint of exactly what we want to see happen in our lives. "Visualization is important," says Saint Germain. "Without it nothing shall appear."

"If you wish more vitality, you must visualize yourself already having that vitality—your muscles rippling with

God's energy, your mind brimming over with vital ideas, tingling with life and light and love," he says. "You must feel and know that the energies of God are flowing through your fingertips and toes, emanating into space the glow of abundant health and a transfiguring countenance.

"As you proceed with this exercise, there will be produced, without additional effort on your part, a beneficial effect upon those whom you contact. But you must be very careful not to seek recognition for this service; otherwise, as it is written in the Book of Life, 'ye have no reward of your Father which is in heaven.'"

I have found that we can maximize the effectiveness of our prayers and meditations by summoning the power of our inner vision. My prayers always include moving pictures of what I am praying for.

In your daily prayers and meditations, try visualizing, as if on a movie screen, the desired outcome of your prayers. See taking place before your eyes what you need to accomplish in every area of your life, including career, education, family, home, health, relationships and spirituality.

Visualize the resolution of difficult situations. If you are working with a special master or angel in your prayers, see him or her interceding on your behalf. Visualize the violet flame consuming all obstacles to your spiritual and material prosperity—whether these obstacles take the form of bounced checks, problems in relationships or discouragement.

Be as specific as possible in your visualizations—and have fun with them. The more centered, concentrated and creative you are, the better your results will be.

PRACTICE THE SCIENCE OF THE IMMACULATE CONCEPT

All that we are is the result of what we have thought.

—Gautama Buddha

The real voyage of discovery consists not in seeking new landscapes, but in having new eyes.

—Marcel Proust

Another key to creative abundance is practicing the science of the immaculate concept. The immaculate concept is the pure concept or image of the soul's potential. To practice the immaculate concept means to hold in mind the highest vision of good for ourselves and others.

Mother Mary has taught me that the science of the immaculate concept is based on the visualization of a perfect idea, which then becomes a magnet that attracts the creative energies of Spirit to one's being to fulfill the pattern held in mind. She says that when we keep our thoughts anchored to the image of the great spiritual being that we are, that image repels all that opposes the manifestation of our reality.

What image do you have of yourself?

Take time to ask yourself that question and to write down what comes to mind. Be honest, because only you are going to see this testimony.

If you list a lot of qualities that are less than positive, realize that you are attracting that less-than-positive image to yourself—because every day of your life you are creating who you are. Whatever you visualize yourself to be, you will become.

Do you see only your flaws and weaknesses, or do you see the beauty of your heart?

Do you see yourself as you imagine others imagine you to be, or do you think of yourself as a soul and spirit with vast potential?

Feedback from others is important, because we don't always realize how we come across to other people. As the Scottish poet Robert Burns wrote, "O wad some power the giftie gie us, to see oursel's as others see us!" It is truly a gift to be able to see ourselves through the eyes of another. Yet we do ourselves a disservice if we look at ourselves exclusively from the outside in.

There is a middle way. That middle way is to see your soul reflecting the image of your inner Christ and your inner Buddha. It is essential that you walk around with the self-image not only of who you are right now, but of who your divine self is—a reflection of God.

Jesus commanded us: "Be ye therefore perfect, even as your Father which is in heaven is perfect." There is a part of us that recognizes the spiritual being that we are and that we can become more of each day. There is also a part of us—the inner child that has been wounded or hurt many times over—that lacks self-worth and tends to devalue the spiritual flame that is at work deep within us.

As you strive to understand, heal and stand up for your sensitive inner child, you can affirm the potential of your shining soul with these affirmations or others that you create.

---— ∞ —---

AFFIRMATIONS:

O ~~Lord~~ God, I AM perfect, even as ~~my~~ you are ~~Father which is in heaven is~~ perfect!

∞

I AM, I AM beholding All,
Mine eye is single as I call;

The Science of the Immaculate Concept

Raise me now and set me free,
Thy holy image now to be.

I AM God's perfection manifest
  in body, mind and soul—
I AM God's direction flowing
  to heal and make me whole!

I AM God's perfect image:
  My form is charged by love;
Let shadows now diminish,
  Be blessed by Comfort's Dove!

Holding the immaculate concept for
yourself—and for everyone around you
—is a spiritual science that can transform your life and your relationships. It's

the real meaning of being your brother's keeper.

"How helpful we can be to one another by holding the immaculate concept for each one's life plan," says Saint Germain. "Let all, in being their brother's keeper, esteem the highest and best possibilities for everyone."

The master El Morya wrote the following prayer to help us hold the immaculate concept for ourselves and others. Each time you say "I AM" in this prayer, you are referring to your divine self and are therefore affirming "God in me is…"

PRAYER:

In the name of my own beloved I AM Presence, I decree:

The Science of the Immaculate Concept

O "I AM Eye" within my soul,
  Help me to see like thee;
May I behold the perfect plan
  Whose power sets all free.

No double vision fills my sight,
  The way is pure and clear;
I AM the viewer of the Light,
  The ~~Christ~~ of all appears.
      God

I AM the eye that God does use
  To see the plan divine;
Right here on earth his way I choose,
  His concept I make mine.

          God
O loving ~~Christ~~, thou living Light,
  Help me to keep thy trust;
I AM thy concept ever right
  So see like thee I must.

CLEAR YOUR SUBCONSCIOUS

There is no room for God in
him who is full of himself.
                    —Hasidic saying

Some people diligently practice the keys to abundance and still don't get the results they want. They climb just so far and then hit a ceiling. Why? Because they haven't cleared their subconscious and they haven't invited God to be part of their plan.

Say you decide to start affirming and believing: "I AM a successful_____
_____"—you fill in the blank.

But if you've been telling yourself for twenty years or twenty lifetimes that you're a failure, your subconscious is going to take some convincing. It's going to say, "I don't believe you."

Our subconscious is like a recording machine. It records every impression we have absorbed throughout our life and our past lives—the good and the bad. And, to our detriment, that includes the negatives we have heard and believed about ourselves.

Every time you think something negative about yourself, every time someone criticizes or intimidates you, your subconscious records the event. Sometimes we don't realize how much we have been influenced by another's thoughts or words, especially a parent, sibling or authority figure. These negatives are booby traps that can undermine our abundance.

For instance, all too often we limit ourselves by our current circumstances—our job, our income, our educational level, our IQ—and what we think we are able to accomplish. We say to ourselves, "My income is thus and such. I have this much social security. My job gives me this much pay, so in ten years I can go just so high."

We have so pigeonholed ourselves and encased ourselves in these boxes that we cancel out the abundant sense of the soul. In the highest dimensions of spirit, however, our soul knows no boundaries. And it wants to be liberated from the tyranny of negative subconscious programming.

The subconscious not only records negative impressions but, like a tape player on automatic replay, it plays back the recordings of the past. It takes hard work to erase these "records." We may need the guidance of a trained psychologist who can help us heal the pain of our wounded inner child.

We may also need to reprogram our subconscious with positive messages. That's what positive affirmations are all about—affirming the innate beauty and positive potential of the soul.

But whatever steps we take, we can accelerate our healing when we accompany them with spiritual work. I have had the best results in clearing the subconscious of negative records by using mantras and affirmations to the violet flame.*

Ask your Higher Self to direct the violet flame into the specific thoughts, actions and words that produced the negative recordings in your subconscious. Visualize the violet flame literally burning up these records, one by one.

Another key for working with your subconscious is to ask your divine self to take dominion over the four components of the mind: the subconscious mind, the conscious mind, the unconscious mind and the superconscious mind.

By doing this we seal our subconscious and unconscious so they do not become tyrants over our soul. We also empower our divine self to generate

---

*See pages 21, 97– 99.

positive energies and impluses in the subconscious and unconscious.

What are these four compartments of the mind? The superconscious mind is the mind of infinite intelligence within us, the all-knowing Mind of God that works through our highest self. The conscious mind is the reasoning mind.

Spiritually speaking, the subconscious mind corresponds to our desires— and that is why it is so influential. This powerful storehouse of energy will bring to fruition your desires, whatever they are.

When it is polluted, the subconscious can do us incalculable harm. When it is cleared and functioning in a healthy way, the subconscious acts like a resilient trampoline, catapulting our highest aspirations into action.

The unconscious mind is the deepest level of our being and can exercise great power over us, although it is not directly accessible to our awareness. Freud said the unconscious includes our primordial wishes and impulses as well as memories and drives we are no longer conscious of but which can have dramatic effects on our thoughts and actions. The unconscious contains the absolutes of Good and Evil.

You can seal the compartments of your mind by directing your I AM Presence to occupy and take dominion over your unconscious and superconscious minds and directing your Holy Christ Self to occupy and take dominion over your subconscious and conscious minds.

The I AM Presence is that portion

of your spiritual self that is the absolute perfection of your divine reality. It is the personal presence of Spirit that abides with you. Your Holy Christ Self is the mediator between you and your I AM Presence. The Holy Christ Self, also known as the Higher Self, is your inner teacher and voice of conscience.

When we place the levels of our mind under the dominion of our I AM Presence and Holy Christ Self, and when we accompany this with the necessary spiritual and psychological work, these dynamic components of our being will produce only good.

—— ∽ ——

PRAYER:

O Mighty I AM Presence, enter now, occupy and take dominion over my superconscious and unconscious minds!

O Holy Christ Self, enter now, occupy and take dominion over my conscious and subconscious minds!

—— ∽ ——

Once you have offered this prayer (preferably once a day), you can recite your own creative affirmations for spiritual and material abundance. It is a good idea to recite your affirmations for each compartment of the mind, as in the following example.

---∞---

AFFIRMATIONS:

In the name of my I AM Presence and Holy ~~Christ Self,~~ *Light is Present in* ~~I AM perfect~~ abundance in my superconscious mind!

In the name of my I AM Presence and Holy ~~Christ Self,~~ *Light is present in* ~~I AM perfect~~ abundance in my conscious mind!

In the name of my I AM Presence and Holy ~~Christ Self,~~ *Light is present in* ~~I AM perfect~~ abundance in my subconscious mind!

In the name of my I AM Presence and Holy ~~Christ Self,~~ *Light is Present* ~~I AM perfect~~ abundance in my unconscious mind!

---∞---

When you begin to dig in and work on your subconscious, don't be surprised or upset if you see the negatives popping out more intensely and more frequently. The more faith, determination and joy you have, the more spiritual light you will generate. This brighter light will naturally expose the blocks to your spiritual progress—the maladies of the spirit that must go.

If you consistently recite prayers and affirmations to the violet flame, such as those I have given in this book, you will get results. Believing and sustaining the affirmations of our soul's success in the face of all woe—this is what it takes to make us whole.

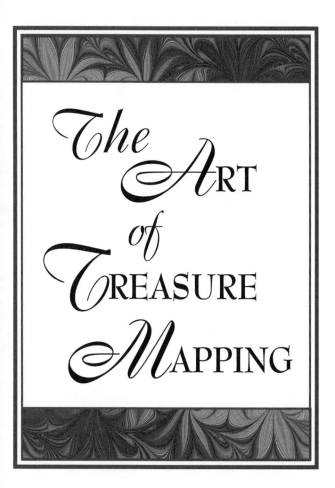

The Art
of
Treasure
Mapping

Destiny is not a matter of chance, it is a matter of choice.

—William Jennings Bryan

A treasure map is a prayer in pictures. You can use it to catch your favorite dreams, shape them into tangible goals and launch them into reality.

Put another way, a treasure map is a blueprint of the spiritual and material abundance you want to create in your life. Like all good maps, it provides direction and helps you stay focused on your destination.

This section offers some basic principles you can use to design an effective treasure map. You can incorporate a few of these ideas or all of them, as your time allows.

To maximize your results, use your treasure map along with the other principles in this book, especially the nine steps to precipitation and the meditation on the creation of the cloud, which appear after this chapter.

If you haven't composed an overall mission statement for your life, I suggest you seriously think about it. All the components of your treasure map will fall under that umbrella vision.

DESIGNING YOUR DREAM THEMES

The world makes way for a man
who knows where he is going.
—Ralph Waldo Emerson

Plan your treasure map before you create it. First, make a list of the dreams you want to see come true in each area of your life. Your list can cover career, finances, family, children, education, health, home, relationships, spirituality, travel and hobbies.

You can also create a collective treasure map with others who are working with you on a joint venture, whether it is your team at work, your family, or a group of friends or colleagues. In that case, your list of dreams would apply to your team's project.

A treasure map is a focus of your highest aspirations. So when making your list don't set limits to your imagination, for it is the universal source of abundance that will be filling your needs, not your human self.

⌇

Allow God to inspire and guide you. "The true alchemist," advises Saint Germain, "begins his experiment by communing with himself and his God in order to perceive the inspiring thoughts of the radiant mind of his Creator."

Before you place images of your

goals on your treasure map, ask God to show you which of your desires are God's desires for you. You want to be sure that what you pour your best energy into is what God would invest his energy in.

∿

Put first things first. Sometimes people use treasure mapping to become financially successful, but they are not spiritually fulfilled. First and foremost, be sure your treasure map includes your spiritual goals. As the Taoist sage Lao Tzu said, "Money or happiness: which is more valuable?...If your happiness depends on money, you will never be happy with yourself."

I also believe that we should be able to justify what we put on our treasure map. Ask only for the things you really need to fulfill your life's purpose. When practicing the keys to abundance, keep in mind that you are working with the laws of energy. And, as Saint Germain says, we are "fully responsible for each use or abuse of energy" within our world. You can actually create negative karma if you use the energy at your disposal to create things you don't need.

I have come to realize that whatever we desire *will* eventually come to us. We magnetize it to ourselves. So take care to set your sail in the right direction. Take time to question your motives and evaluate your desires. And if God puts more resources at your disposal than you asked for, it is because he wants you to lovingly give your abundance to others who are in greater need than you.

~

Work with God and your Higher Self to refine your ideas. In his nine steps to precipitation, Saint Germain teaches us to let our Higher Mind help design and perfect our ideas.

Take time to converse with God and commune with your Higher Self. Listen to the voice of God within and watch for signs that God may give you. Once you are certain about what you need, then you are ready to construct your treasure map.

Even after you have designed your map, don't be concerned if you need to modify it a day later or a week later. Your treasure map is meant to be a work in progress.

CAPTURE YOUR DREAMS ON PAPER

A goal is a dream with a deadline.
—Leo B. Helzel

*Y*our treasure map may be large or small. You can post it on a wall or door or craft it in a notebook.

If you choose to post your map on a wall or door, use posterboard so that you can easily paste or tape pictures onto it. Choose a color for the board that you really like. You'll be meditating on your map at least twice a day, so you want to make it as appealing as possible.

∽

You can picture several goals on one map or create more than one map, each dedicated to a different need. For some people, a scrapbook works better because you can dedicate each page to something new.

I learned about the power of a scrapbook as a treasure map from my late husband and teacher, Mark Prophet. When I was sorting through Mark's belongings after he passed on, I found a scrapbook that he had never shown me. It was yellowed with age and he had probably not looked at it for years. I think he had made it while he was in the Air Force, years before I ever met him.

Mark had cut out pictures from magazines from the 1940s and put them in this scrapbook. He had a picture of his dream house with a white picket fence around it. He placed this house in Colorado Springs, where he had been stationed in the Air Force. Years later, this dream of Mark's came true when we moved our headquarters to a beautiful property in Colorado Springs.

In his scrapbook, Mark also had a picture of the ideal woman he wanted to marry. What really touched my heart was that the picture he had cut out of a magazine looked just like me. So the treasure map worked for Mark, and it can work for you too.

∽

Divide your map or scrapbook into sections for each area of your

life. Then choose images and statements that show exactly what you want to accomplish in that area of endeavor.

⤳

Always picture something better than the best of what you are experiencing now. You always want to be reaching for something higher.

⤳

Be precise when selecting images and statements for your map. Show and tell exactly what you want, including size, dimension, color, location and deadlines.

For example, when portraying the finances you need, put on your map money, pictures of gold coins or a check made out to you for the specific amount needed. If you need a new car or house, write out all the features you require and, if possible, use an exact picture of what you want. On the career section of your map, you can show someone practicing your desired profession.

Don't forget to state by what date you want to see your goals accomplished and the exact location where you want your dreams to come true.

In 1961, when Mark Prophet and I were searching for a headquarters for The Summit Lighthouse,[1] we looked all over Washington, D.C. Then we looked in Maryland and in Virginia, and we still couldn't find what we wanted. We were praying about this, and finally we asked God why we couldn't find the right place. The answer came flashing back: we needed to be more specific.

Because we still had a nebulous idea of what we needed, we were getting nowhere. Once we sat down and defined exactly what we wanted, where we wanted it, when we wanted it and how much money we needed to buy it, the whole thing came together.

⌒

Use colored pictures and images on your map. The imagination responds well to color.

⌒

An effective way to arrange your treasure map is according to the "bagua," a pattern that is derived from the I Ching and is used in the

Oriental art of feng shui. The bagua is an archetypal pattern of universal and personal change. It is shaped like an octagon and it depicts the movement of energy, or ch'i, in the eight areas of life.

Feng shui is the art of arranging our external environment to create harmony and balance in our life. The ancients who practiced feng shui knew that our outer surroundings mirror the conditions of our life, and vice versa. They therefore taught that by arranging our surroundings to be in harmony with the natural order, we can achieve happiness and prosperity. This is where the bagua comes into play.

All of our space—our home, each room in it, our office, our desk, our yard, our car—is an extension and reflection of ourselves. Since this is so, we can superimpose the bagua pattern over any space to diagnose what is happening in our worlds. And by focusing on each of the eight sections of that space, we can

Abundance Blessings	Fame Enlightenment	Partnerships Love Marriage
Health Family		Children Creativity
Knowledge Self-knowledge Spirituality	Career	Helpful friends Travel

Bagua map used in feng shui

influence what happens in the corresponding department of our life.

Applying this to treasure mapping, we can overlay the bagua pattern onto our personal treasure map and place pictures of our goals in the corresponding sections. To superimpose the bagua over your treasure map, line up the bottom of your map with the bottom of the bagua.

Feng shui also teaches that clutter blocks the flow of energy. If a certain space is cluttered, energy will stagnate and there may be blockages in the part of our life corresponding to that space. Conversely, when we enhance and beautify a certain space, we increase the flow of energy to the corresponding area of our life.

Take some time to evaluate what's

happening in the eight areas of your life outlined in the bagua. Is there a blockage somewhere? Are things at a standstill?

Now take a look at your environment—your home, your rooms, your workplace, even your garage. Is the energy free to circulate or does it stagnate because of clutter?

Sometimes a healthy spring-cleaning is just what we need to rejuvenate our spiritual, mental, emotional and physical worlds. Of course, feng shui goes into much greater detail and subtlety, but with these basic principles we can begin to increase the flow of spiritual and material abundance into our lives.

We can also relate the clutter principle to our treasure maps. If we create a clear and uncluttered treasure map arranged according to the bagua pattern, and we portray exactly what we want in each section, then energy can flow more freely to form the patterns of our desires.

What about the center of the map? Some systems of feng shui place the T'ai Chi in the center. The T'ai Chi is the Chinese symbol that represents the harmonious interaction and integration of the yin (female) and yang (male) forces in the universe.

The center of the bagua and of your treasure map represents unity. It is the hub that integrates all the other sections. The center is also the place where we reenergize before the seeds we have planted begin to blossom. It is the point of rest and renewal before the next surge of growth.

So what should we picture in the center of our maps? It depends on the purpose of the map. If your map has one primary focus, you could put a picture of that focus in the center. If the timing of your goal is all-important, then your target date could be in the center. You might prefer to put something in the middle that depicts your center, your hub—maybe your mission statement or a symbol of your spiritual source or your spiritual self. Be creative and imaginative!

⌐

To further stimulate the flow of energy to your endeavors, you can post your treasure map in the section of your house or the section of a room that, according to the bagua map,

represents what you are focusing on.

When superimposing the bagua over a house or a room, the front door or the door to the room would open into the bottom part of the map. In other words, the door would open into some part of the bottom line of knowledge, career and helpful friends.

Here's how it would work. If you are concentrating on your finances, for instance, you could post your financial treasure map in the wealth section of your house or your room (the back left corner). You could place a treasure map for relationships in the partnership section of your house or room (the back right corner).

⤳

Put pictures of one or more ascended masters on your treasure map. The ascended masters are the saints and sages of East and West who have become one with God. They sponsor our endeavors and work behind the scenes of life to help us.

Pictures of your favorite masters will remind you that they are your partners and are working with you to help you accomplish your goals.

∽

If you are able to go into this level of detail, you can **place successive pictures of yourself over periods of time accomplishing your goals.** You can create a timeline showing what you want immediately and what you want to accomplish in later periods of your life.

∽

Accompany your images with words and affirmations describing your needs. I suggest you write your goals out as affirmations. You can also preface them with a prayer to your I AM Presence and Holy Christ Self so that you are affirming the completion of your goals by the power of the God within you.

So you would say, for instance, "In the name of my I AM Presence and Holy Christ Self, I AM compassionate," or "In the name of my I AM Presence and Holy Christ Self, I AM successful at_____" or "I am completing my master's degree in _____."

∽

Create images or statements of what you will offer to God in return for the blessings you are asking for. In reality, we never get something for nothing. Every bit of energy that God gives us "costs" something.

The divine law is clear: when we give to life, we receive from life. If we stop giving of ourselves, we will stop receiving. I have found that we are, in fact, expected to give more to the universe than we are asking for.

You may want to write a letter to God to accompany your treasure map. In the letter, state what you will do in return for divine assistance, such as volunteering to work with the disadvantaged or elderly, tending the sick or adopting children.

We are saying, "Please help me accomplish this goal, God, and in exchange I will do this for you." But be realistic. Don't pledge more than you can give. Once you have written the letter, keep a copy as a reminder of your pledge and then burn the original.

∽

Don't clutter your map with too many pictures and affirmations. Make several maps if you find that you have too much on one map.

∽

Unless you are making a treasure map with a group for a collective need, **keep your map private. Put it in a place where there is positive and uplifting energy.** For instance, don't put it in a part of your house that visitors frequent, and don't put it where someone who is cynical about your plans will be able to view it.

MAKING YOUR DREAMS A REALITY

If you can dream it, you can do it.
—Walt Disney

$\mathcal{O}$nce you have created and posted your treasure map, meditate on your map at least twice a day, perhaps in the morning and before you go to bed at night. As you do so, read your affirmations aloud. Reinforce them by feeling and believing that you have already attained your goals. If you have a group or family treasure map, repeat the affirmations with those who are part of your alliance.

Repetition is important for the subconscious mind. It reinforces our healthy desires. Every time you repeat an affirmation, the conscious mind plants the seed and the subconscious waters it.

～

Consciously turn your requests over to God and ask him to fulfill them according to his will.

Remember that it is God who will do the real work of fulfilling your requests, even though you may be the instrument that he works through. For as Moses told the Israelites, "Do not say to yourself, 'My power and the might of my own hand have gotten me this wealth.' But remember the LORD your

God, for it is he who gives you power to get wealth."

∽

Keep an ongoing dialogue with God. Amidst the hustle and bustle of your day, take a little time to talk to God. And remember, prayer is a two-way street—don't forget to listen to his reply. Synergy with the sacred is the key to creative abundance.

∽

Don't be attached to the out-come of your requests and don't anticipate how your desires will be fulfilled. That's up to God to decide.

If we have a one-track mind, we limit our options. When we are overly attached or anxious, we aren't open to surprise packages or new opportunities that may be right under our noses. Sometimes God finds a better way to fill our needs than we anticipated.

~

Pour your whole heart into making your dreams come true. Take the necessary steps to get the ball rolling. We all get what we want out of life as long as we really want it and are committed to getting it.

~

Supplement your meditations on your treasure map with violet-flame affirmations and mantras to transmute the karma that blocks the materialization of your dreams.

The X factor in getting the spiritual

and material abundance we need is always karma. We may want to go in a certain direction, but our karma takes us into byways that seem to be off the beaten track of our mission.

Yet dealing with karma is always our first priority. Every day another bundle of the negative karma we have created in the past is delivered to our doorstep for resolution. Maybe we experience that karma as a breakdown of our car or a breakdown of a relationship. Things just don't seem to move the way they should.

The violet flame is like oil in the gears; it makes things run more smoothly. Along with service and devotion to God, it can help us transmute the negative karma that could interfere with our mission.

The Art of Treasure Mapping

I can remember when all I knew about my purpose in life was that I had to do something for God and that I had to find out what it was. Since I didn't know what it was, it became my mission to find out. So each day as I was growing up, I would pursue those things that I thought would lead me closer to discovering what my mission was.

When I finally discovered my mission, my greatest desire was to be free of the encumbrances that would prevent me from fulfilling it. I realized that those encumbrances were karma as well as elements of my psychology.

I realized that if I was serious about fulfilling my mission, I would have to transmute that karma with the violet flame and work on resolving those issues in my psychology. I also realized that I would have to develop greater self-mastery so I could deal with the challenges to my mission. This is the kind of work we need to dig into if we really want to make the most of our opportunities for creative abundance.

∽

Remember your pledges to God. Give back to God what you promised. Don't wait until you get results to start giving. Start fulfilling your end of the bargain right away.

∽

Update your treasure map as needed. If you need a new map, it's a good sign! It means you're making progress. You've either accomplished your first set of goals or you've refined your sense of where you want to go and how you want to get there.

If you need to make a new map, burn your old one, get out a new poster-board and turn to page 55.

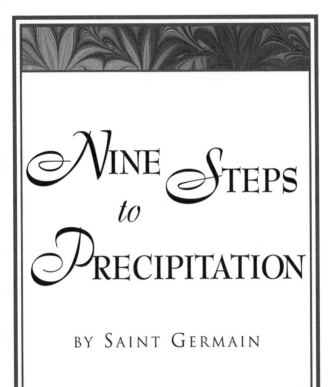

Nine Steps to Precipitation

to

Precipitation

by Saint Germain

———— ∞ ————

Who can set bounds to the possibilities of man?...Man has access to the entire mind of the Creator, is himself the creator in the finite.
    —Ralph Waldo Emerson

Alchemy is the science of the mystic and it is the forte of the self-realized man who, having sought, has found himself to be one with God and is willing to play his part.
    —Saint Germain

 —— ∞ ——

Nine Steps to Precipitation

1. Light is the alchemical key! The words "**Let there be light**" are the first fiat of the creation and the first step in proper precipitation.

AFFIRMATIONS:

Let there be light!
Let there be light where I AM THAT I AM!

2. **Create a mind blueprint of the object you wish to produce.** This should incorporate definite size, proportion, substance, density, color and quality in detailed picture form.

Let each student of alchemy recognize that he has within himself a Higher

Mind that is capable of holding patterns of infinite dimensions. This Mind functions independently of the outer mind without human restriction of any kind.

Acquire the habit of consciously giving to this blessed Higher Mind, or Christ Self, the responsibility for designing and perfecting the embryonic ideas and patterns of your creation. For many of these patterns, which at first appeared to be consciously conceived by the alchemist, frequently have their origin within this higher portion of the blessed Self.

Remember, twenty-four hours of each day your Higher Mind is active in expanded dimensions. This blessed Comforter, unknown and unexperienced by you outwardly, waits to be called

May we have your comments on this book?

We hope that you have enjoyed this book and that it will occupy a special place in your library. It would be helpful to us in meeting your needs and the needs of our readers if you would fill out and mail this postage-free card to us.

Book title: _____

Your comments: _____

_____

_____

How did this book come to your attention? _____

How would you rate this book on a scale of 1 to 5, with 5 being the highest? _____

Topics of interest to you: _____

Would you like to receive a free catalog of our publications? ☐ Yes ☐ No

Name _____ Address _____

City _____ State _____ Zip Code _____ Phone no. _____

E-mail: _____

(We will not make your name available to other companies.)

Thank you for taking the time to give us your feedback.

Call us toll free at 1-800-245-5445. Outside the U.S.A., call 406-848-9500. Summit University Press titles are available from fine bookstores everywhere. E-mail: info@summituniversitypress.com www.summituniversitypress.com

491-CA R8/01

SUMMIT
UNIVERSITY
PRESS®

Publisher of fine
spiritual books
since 1975

BUSINESS REPLY MAIL
FIRST-CLASS MAIL   PERMIT NO. 20   GARDINER MT

POSTAGE WILL BE PAID BY ADDRESSEE

SUMMIT UNIVERSITY PRESS®
PO Box 5000
Gardiner, MT 59030-9900

into action and does function free of ordinary space/time limitations.

Employ your Higher Mind, then, both as your apprentice and as your teacher; for the Holy Spirit of truth moving therein can lead you into all truth!

——————— ∞ ———————

AFFIRMATION:

I AM life of God-direction,
Blaze thy light of truth in me.
Focus here all God's perfection,
From all discord set me free.

Make and keep me anchored ever
In the justice of thy plan—
I AM the presence of perfection
Living the life of God in man!

(give three times)

——————— ∞ ———————

3. Determine where you wish the object to manifest.

4. If you know the material substance of which it is composed, memorize its atomic pattern. If not, call to the Divine Intelligence within your Higher Mind to register the pattern for you from the Universal Intelligence and impress it upon your memory body and your mind.

5. Call for light to take on the atomic pattern you are holding, to coalesce around that pattern and then to "densify" into form.

6. Call for the multiplication of this atomic structure until molecules of substance begin to fill the void occupying

the space in which you desire the object to appear.

7. When the total outline is filled with the vibratory action of the fourth-dimensional substance representing the desired manifestation, **ask for the full lowering of the atomic density into three-dimensional form and substance within the pattern established by the matrix of your mind.**

8. **When the visualization of the blueprint within your mind is complete, immediately seal it.** Do not think that by sealing your plan you are closing the door to the improvement of its design. Improvements can be made in subsequent models. The words **"It is**

finished!" are therefore the second fiat of creation following "Let there be light!"

The call of beloved Jesus at the hour of his greatest testing, **"Nevertheless, not my will, but thine, be done,"** when spoken at the moment of the sealing of the matrix, ensures that the guiding forces of power, wisdom and love will amend the precipitated pattern where necessary in order that the more perfect designs of the Creator may come forth.

This provides man with the added benefit of the assistance of the Almighty as he forms and develops his own idea-pattern of destiny in accordance with cosmic purpose.

Protect your experiment by guarded action and guarded meditation. Your visualization of a blue

light around yourself, your matrix and its manifestation will serve to focalize the desired protection.

AFFIRMATIONS:

It is finished!

Nevertheless, not my will, but thine, be done.

I AM God's will manifest everywhere,
I AM God's will perfect beyond
 compare,
I AM God's will so beautiful and fair,
I AM God's willing bounty everywhere.

9A. Now that you have created a thought matrix and sealed it against the intrusion of impinging mind radiation from others, protect your creative intent and, as Jesus said, "Go and **tell no man.**" This law of precipitation allows you to circumvent concentrated beams of human thought and feeling patterns, which can be most disturbing to a successful alchemical experiment.

Avoid, then, the dissipation of energy by the intrusion of a multiplicity of minds, except where two or more individuals are specifically cooperating in joint precipitation.

9B. **Await results.** Do not be tense if your manifestation is not immediate or if after a reasonable length of time it appears that results are not forthcoming. Despair destroys the very faith upon which your experiment is built. You must **hold your faith** as you hold the gossamer veil composing the mental image.

If you have spent years in the grip of human emotions, **these records must be consumed by the alchemical fires of the violet flame** to make way for the nobler ideas and forms you would image forth.

———— ∞ ————

AFFIRMATIONS:

Violet fire, thou love divine,
Blaze within this heart of mine!
Thou art mercy forever true,
Keep me always in tune with you.

(give three times)

Creative Abundance

✧

I AM Light, thou Christ in me,
Set my mind forever free;
Violet fire, forever shine
Deep within this mind of mine.

God who gives my daily bread,
With violet fire fill my head
Till thy radiance heavenlike
Makes my mind a mind of light.

(give three times)

✧

I AM the hand of God in action,
Gaining victory every day;
My pure soul's great satisfaction
Is to walk the Middle Way.

(give three times)

✧

Nine Steps to Precipitation

Beloved I AM Presence bright,
Round me seal your tube of light
From ascended master flame
Called forth now in God's own name.
Let it keep my temple free
From all discord sent to me.

I AM calling forth violet fire
To blaze and transmute all desire,
Keeping on in freedom's name
Till I AM one with the violet flame.
(give three times)

And in full faith I consciously accept this manifest, manifest, manifest! (three times) right here and now with full power, eternally sustained, all-powerfully active, ever expanding and world enfolding until all are wholly ascended in

the light and free! Beloved I AM!
Beloved I AM! Beloved I AM!

9C. **To your new ideas you must give
your time and your energy.**

**How important is the service of
ordered prayer.** Prayer opens the door of
God's intervention in human affairs. It
provides an avenue whereby the ascended masters and cosmic beings who desire
to serve the planet earth can render special assistance because they have been
called upon to do so. For the law decrees
that the heavenly hosts must be peti-
tioned by some among mankind, must
be invited to intervene, before they are
permitted to intercede on behalf of hu-
manity.

To the alchemist the value of prayer is manifold. In addition to the aforesaid benefits, it provides an impetus to enhance his values and further the goal of divine truth while the mental mold is in the process of coming into physical manifestation.

Remember, this is divine artistry of the highest type. It is also co-creation with God and, as such, is best used by those whose purposes parallel the divine. Thus, when the will of man is aligned with the will of God, the light of God does not fail to precipitate that will in the fullness of time, space and opportunity.

Alchemists of the sacred fire, here is the sacred cosmic formula:

Theos = God

Rule = Law

You = Being

Theos + Rule + You = God's law active as Principle within your being (*TRY*).

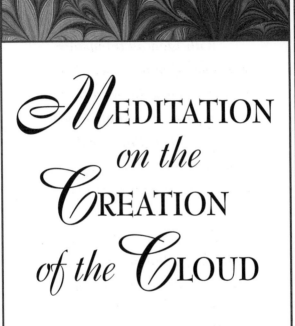

Meditation on the Creation of the Cloud

by Saint Germain

— ∞ —

With God all things are possible! If you possess his consciousness, then all things are, in fact, immediately possible to you. If this is not your instantaneous experience, then you need more of his consciousness....

The cloud, as the manifestation of the power of your creative energy, the fire of your Spirit, will draw into your world the very consciousness of God himself.

—Saint Germain

— ∞ —

One of the most effective means by which change can be produced is through what I will call "the creation of the cloud." I am referring to a cloud of infinite energy that is everywhere present but nowhere manifest until it is called into action.

Throughout this ritual your consciousness must be kept pure, charged with love, aware of the infinite potential of the cosmic mind of God and completely identified with all constructive momentums. Remember that it is practice that makes perfect, that it is motive that transfigures design, that it is beauty that transfixes the soul.

1. **Stand now before your altar, honoring the living God** and his fiat "Take dominion!" You are about to create, and you will first create the cloud from the enormous power of God stored at every point in space, waiting to be invoked.

2. **We shall create in our minds first a milky white radiance,** and we shall see this milky white radiance as an electronic vibratory action of vital, moving, ineffable light. The concentration of the light is that which makes the milky white color.

3. Having created in our minds this form of a bright translucent cloud, we **allow it to enfold our physical bodies and to occupy our forcefield.** For a

moment we become lost in the midst of the cloud, and then it seems as though it has always been there. Its atmosphere is familiar, comfortable.

4. **Let this bright and shining cloud at first be nine feet in diameter around oneself.** Later, perhaps, we shall expand it to a diameter of ninety feet, then nine hundred feet and further.

In our early meditations we shall **concentrate on intensifying the action of the white light in our minds.** Once we have developed the sense of this cloud being around our physical forms, we shall understand that whereas the cloud can be made visible to the physical sight, our primary concern is to keep its high vibratory action purely spiritual.

5. Those of you who are familiar with electronics and the workings of a rheostat will understand that by a simple twist of the dial of consciousness, we can **intensify the vibratory action of the cloud. We coalesce more light around each central point of light;** for our cloud is composed of many light points whose auras diffuse and blend with one another, making the total effect one of a lacy yet highly concentrated white radiance, a pure swirling cloud of cosmic energy.

We are amplifying an intense action of the light from within its own forcefield —more than would normally manifest in a given area. We are thereby drawing upon universal God-power to produce this cloud. **It first penetrates and then hallows our immediate forcefield in** order that we may have a spiritual altar upon which we may project the pictures of reality that we desire to create.

6. **This cloud can be used therapeutically** for the healing of the nations and the soul of a planet. You can also use it as a platform to invoke, as Christ did upon the Mount of Transfiguration, the presence of the ascended masters to assist you in your alchemical experiments and in your ministrations to life.

Where you are yet ignorant of just what you ought to produce for yourself and others, you can, in a gentle, child-like manner, ask God to produce out of the great pool of his light-energy the miracle of his healing love, not only in your life and in the lives of your loved ones, but also in the lives of the multitudes in the world at large.

You can ask the power of God and of the kingdom of heaven to come into manifestation upon earth. You can ask for the golden age to be born, for an end to strife and struggle. You can ask for love to take dominion over the world.

If you will open your heart to the needs of the world and to the love of the Divine Mother that seeks expression through your uplifted consciousness, limitless ideas for universal service will flow into your mind.

7. **Ask God to increase the potential of the cloud by giving the following prayer.**

———— ∞ ————

PRAYER:

In the name of the Father and of the Son and of the Holy Spirit, I command billions of points of light to now expand, gather more of the sacred fire, increase the mighty potential of the fiery cloud, and be the brilliance, the vital, moving, ineffable light of Almighty God—even that light of the cloud of my own Mighty I AM Presence—where I AM!

By the authority of the universal law of God, I decree this holy thing, O God. I accept it done in the name of my own beloved Christ Self. And, behold, I see it done, and it is done where I AM.

Christ Self of me, hold the vision, train the eye of God upon it, and let me know and experience this expansion! For indeed, I AM the cloud. The cloud is in me.

I AM the highly concentrated white radiance.

I AM the cause behind the effect of the cloud.

I AM the magnet of the Great Central Sun within my heart, magnetizing the cloud of infinite energy where I AM.

I AM a pure, swirling cloud of cosmic energy!

8. Assign this radiant cloud of brilliant energy to a particular purpose with the following prayer.

The Creation of the Cloud

——— ∞ ———

PRAYER:

Lord God Almighty, O Brahman, O Word, I direct this cloud of infinite energy to now be attenuated in or over: *[name location or situation]*.

From the earth, from the sea, high into the upper atmosphere, I AM now the authority of the white-fire cloud in manifestation spiritually. Through the threefold flame of my heart, I AM commanding the crystallization of the cloud from Spirit to Matter.

Let this cloud of God consume now: *[name personal or world conditions in need of healing or resolution]*.

I demand and I AM the release of the radiant cloud of energy.

So be it. It is done. It is finished. It is sealed.

The zeal of the LORD will perform it! Amen.

9. **Once you have held the vision of the cloud and turned it over to your Higher Self to sustain, to the latent God-faculties within you, your God Presence will sustain it for the required period.**

In time you will find that the glow of the cloud will softly suffuse itself through your physical body. As this takes place there will come a sharpening of the mind and a new sense of awareness of all life everywhere.

As you gain spiritual power through

these periods of meditation upon the cloud—which at first should not exceed fifteen minutes a day—understand that **the creative cloud will continue to expand throughout the universe as a globe of translucent white fire**, eddying in ever-widening spheres to contact all that is real and that is really yours.

Secrets of Prosperity

by Mark L. Prophet

Nothing we ever imagined is beyond our powers, only beyond our present self-knowledge
—Theodore Roszak

$\mathcal{J}$n the Bible the Apostle John says, "Beloved, I wish above all things that thou mayest prosper and be in health, even as thy soul prospereth."

Prosperity is abundance. The Lord Christ, when he was teaching in Judea, said, "I AM come that they might have life, and that they might have it more abundantly." Somehow or other people have a habit of misconstruing the Master's intent without really meaning to and thus cutting themselves off from and denying the intention of the Deity.

Now, obviously none of us could subscribe to a share-the-wealth plan where we would pool all the money on the planet into one pot and all wind up with ninety-eight cents. This is about what it would amount to. Yet if we put all the money into a pot and divided it between all the people on earth and gave each person his portion, in a matter of probably seven years just about all the money would be back where it started from.

This is true because the divine distribution of wealth on this planet occurs according to karmic patterns and karmic law. In most cases, every person who has money is entitled to it according to his karma—even if he didn't earn it in one lifetime but it came to him through inheritance or he won the Irish sweepstakes. Money comes to people because there is something in their Causal Body that attracts wealth to their being. And when you practice the laws of prosperity, you create good karma and you therefore begin to attract to yourself prosperity.

FIRST SECRET

NEVER DAM UP THE FLOW OF YOUR ENERGY

---

*T*he possession of money itself does not make a person better or worse. Not at all. Money—like every talent and gift of God—is responsibility. And when you have a great deal of money or even a little money, it is a form of prosperity that should not be dammed up like the Dead Sea.

The River Jordan flows down toward the Dead Sea and empties into it, but there is absolutely no outlet in the Dead Sea. This has been used a lot in Sunday schools to illustrate certain spiritual laws. Whenever you have anything that continually takes in and never gives out, it's a symbol of death or stagnation because there is no flow and there is no movement.

Blood flows through the whole body and returns through the heart for oxygenation in the lungs. We all know that's basic physiology. But here's something that's almost frightening: the moment you dam up an artery, you really have trouble.

Now, you may wonder why I'm bringing this up. Quite a few ladies, and men, too, have had varicose veins.

Doctors can perform an operation for varicose veins where they tie off certain vessels and just stop the flow of blood.

One book written by a doctor who exposes some of the malpractices in hospitals and in the medical profession tells about a woman who had this operation. Two days after the doctor tied this blood vessel off she noticed that her toes were becoming very painful and inflamed. Then she noticed they were turning dark and discolored, and then her whole foot turned discolored. Well, when she went back to the doctor it was too late, and she lost her foot completely. It turned gangrenous because there was no flow of blood into her foot.

I think very few people realize how beautifully nature works to keep our blood flowing through our system. Well, prosperity is just as natural to the children of God as the flow of blood. And one of the ascended masters' secrets of prosperity is that they always let go and never dam up the flow of their energy. Businessmen do the same thing, in a way, by investing and reinvesting their capital.

SECOND SECRET

GIVE TEN PERCENT OF YOURSELF TO GOD

Another secret of prosperity is to give ten percent of yourself to God. There is no law that says you can't give more, but I think to give less is to deplete the seed.

Giving a tenth is what is known as a tithe. Today I received a revelation concerning the word *tithe*. I didn't hear it as *tithe*. I heard it as *tie thee*. The ten percent is the portion of the divine talent that becomes a seed to tie you to your God Presence, to God, the Great Source, so that the next cycle of the decimal system will grow. It's the zero, you see. You come one, two, three, four, five, six, seven, eight, nine, and then you "tie thee"—tie thee to the Presence.

"Tie thee" means a tie, a link, a union with your Source, the source of your supply. And by giving that tenth, you're planting the seed that makes your supply grow into the next cycle. If you deny it to God, you actually don't gain at all. By holding it back you lose, because you don't have any seed to make it grow in the next cycle.

There is a successful construction machinery man who made a compact with God to give away ten percent of all that he had when he was a young man. This man has a huge family and he travels all over the United States working for God. He pays far more attention to God's business than he does to his machinery business. And his machinery business is so big today that it's a tremendous industry. He has always used this secret of prosperity of giving the seed. As a result, his supply has just multiplied and multiplied and multiplied, because the law has continued to work for him.

GIVE IN SECRET

*M*any years ago Lloyd Douglas wrote *Magnificent Obsession*. In this book he revealed one of the great secrets of the masters: keep your mouth shut about what you do. This is why some people come up to me and whisper in my ear and say, "I'll give so much money to your university." They don't want anybody else to hear it, because they know that if they give in secret, their supply will return to them and will also be multiplied.

One of the problems in the modern church has been to publish the names of donors in some of the church literature. In New York City there's a tremendous activity of this kind. They call everybody that gives a donation a sponsor, and then they publish the names of all the sponsors on a list. As Jesus said, "Verily, they have their reward."

There is a place in the Bible where the secret is given: "When you give," Jesus said, "don't sound a trumpet before yourselves as the hypocrites do. But give in secret."

FOURTH SECRET

GIVE SOMETHING, NO MATTER HOW SMALL

*A*nother secret of prosperity is to give of the little bit that thou hast. Some people have very little money. They say,

"Well, I hate to offer The Summit Lighthouse ninety-eight cents; it's too belittling to me." But Mr. Rockefeller gave people only a dime, didn't he? All he gave away to everybody was ten cents. He was always handing out ten cents as his charitable contribution.

So don't feel that it is belittling to give a small amount. God knows exactly what you have. No one else has to know. Look at it this way: it is more blessed to give than it is to receive. And you will receive, because giving is a secret of prosperity. People who dam up the flow by saying, "Oh, I'm afraid," generate fear in their worlds.

USE THE GIFTS GOD HAS GIVEN YOU

*T*his fear was illustrated in the parable of the servant who received one lousy talent. Before his lord left for a far country, he entrusted some of his goods to his servants according to their abilities. To one servant he gave five talents, to another servant he gave two talents and to a third servant he gave one talent. In those days, a talent was a valuable silver coin.

When the lord returned, he wanted to know what they had done with their money. He asked the servant to whom he had given five talents, "How did you do with it?" The man said, "I gained five more talents with the five you gave me."

The lord said, "Well done, thou good and faithful servant: thou hast been faithful over a few things, I will make thee ruler over many things: Enter thou into the joy of thy lord."

The second servant reported that he had doubled his talents as well. Then came the poor little guy who had the one talent. He had wrapped his talent in a napkin and buried it in the earth.

The man pulled that one lousy talent out of the ground, took it out of the old moldy napkin and said to his lord, "Here is exactly what you gave to me. I knew that you were a hard man and I was afraid, my lord, at this awesome responsibility. So I took that one talent which you gave me and I hid it in the earth."

The lord looked at him rather

sternly and quizzically. Then he said: "Thou wicked and slothful servant. Take, therefore, that talent from him and give it unto him which hath ten talents. For unto everyone that hath shall be given, and he shall have abundance: but from him that hath not shall be taken away that which he hath."

This parable has been much maligned and much misunderstood. It has been quoted to show that those who don't have much are going to have less and those who do have are going to have even more. That wasn't what was meant at all. What the parable showed was that the man who had the one talent *but didn't use it* had his talent taken away from him.

Don't ever let anybody fool you about these scriptures, because the secret of prosperity is clearly indicated: use that which thou hast. Do you see the point? It's a lot different than people say. Over half the people who preach about these scriptures don't understand their real meaning.

So, by wisely using our gifts from God we multiply them. This does not have to involve money. Money is merely a medium of exchange. This concept can also involve service. It can involve things you do for others. It can involve other people as well as your immediate family.

THINK OF THE WORLD AS YOUR FAMILY

*O*ne of the things that crystallizes the consciousness and keeps the supply from coming into your world is the feeling of owning people. A lot of people feel that their children or their spouses or their mother or their father or their brother or their sister—in other words, their family—is all-important.

But you don't own people and they don't own you. All people are free. The sense of an exclusive family circle that rules out everybody else in the world is one of the reasons the consciousness crystallizes and prosperity doesn't come in.

Thinking of the world as your

family doesn't mean you have to give a dollar to every beggar that comes along. But when you start feeling and thinking in terms of loving other people outside the family and doing something for someone else—not necessarily someone you love but someone who may even be impersonal to you—you begin to think like God. For God has to take his energy and assistance and give it to people that hate him and that spit upon him.

Do you know there are people who curse God on this planet and mean it? I have heard people damn God and shake their fist in his face and dare him to strike them with lightning. In most cases, God turns around and still pumps breath and life energy into these people. He still takes care of them because he's an impersonal God as well as a personal God.

So one of the greatest secrets of prosperity is to have the ability to detach oneself from personal concerns and to become impersonal. This ability is a magnet that makes you godlike.

SEVENTH SECRET

REMEMBER THAT THE GOD PRESENCE IS THE SOURCE OF YOUR SUPPLY

"I AM come that they might have life, and that they might have it more abundantly" is the secret of it all. The Bible doesn't say, "You have come." It says, "I AM come"—in other words, the I AM, the God in me, is come— "that they might have life, and that they might have it more abundantly." This denotes that the God Presence is the source of your supply. Supply doesn't come from outer sources.

I can tell you a funny story about The Summit Lighthouse. It isn't so funny, but it happens to be true. In our early days, when we were in Washington, D.C., our budget was much less than it is today. I would sometimes wait three or four days to go down to the post office and pick up the mail. Then we would get a good stack and it would seem as if we were getting more money.

This was good for my morale. If I went down there and found only four or five envelopes, it was depressing, especially since we had a lot of bills to pay. So I'd wait and I'd bring home a big stack.

One time I kept track of donations over a period of several months. Whether the mail was a big stack or just half as big or only four letters, the amount of money in the envelopes never seemed to vary more than ten dollars. Now, you figure that one out.

I'd open four envelopes and there would be a hundred dollar bill in one, maybe a fifty in another and a check for seventy-five dollars in another. Those four envelopes would contain as much money as a great big stack of mail.

At other times I'd come home with the mail and I'd say, "Gee, we really got a lot today," but there would be just a dollar in one envelope, fifty cents in another, a dollar in another and a check for a dollar and seventy-five cents in another envelope. One woman sent in a check for seventy-five cents! And it was like that all the way through the big stack of mail.

So I've noticed that the Lord takes care of you regardless of the source. We have experienced this and have found that supply continually comes in.

EIGHTH SECRET

CALL UPON FORTUNA

We have also noticed that the ascended lady master Fortuna possesses the power to release more money when we really need it.

I'm going to tell you one of our secrets: every time we get into trouble and have a contract to meet and we don't have the money to meet it, we get up on this platform and the whole staff gives the decree to Fortuna, "Light's Treasures":

Fortuna, Goddess of Supply,
Of all God's wealth from realms on high,
Release thy treasures from the Sun
And now bestow on everyone

Whose heart beats one with
   God's own light
The power to draw from heaven's height,
Abundance to expand the plan
The masters hold for every man.

Attune our consciousness with thee,
Expand our vision now to see

Secrets of Prosperity

That opulence is meant for all
Who look to God and make the call.

We now demand, we do command
Abundant manna from God's hand,
That now below as is Above
All mankind shall express God's love.

We sometimes recite this decree for ten, fifteen, twenty minutes or a half an hour. Invariably, within a few days the mail will bring in the required amount of money.

DEPEND ON GOD

This means we don't look to people as our source of supply. When I first started this activity with the ascended masters' help, we had a woman worth more than sixteen million dollars in the organization. We thought she was really going to be of great assistance to us— the human thought that. We were never more disappointed in our lives, and probably justly so.

Then we had another angel come along that used to give us a few hundred dollars every month, but she got mad over nothing and quit sending that much money. She's very spasmodic—once in a while we hear from her, but not very often.

We've quit looking to people for our supply. We look completely to God. This is another secret of supply: don't depend on any human being. Depend on God.

My wife, Elizabeth, had a great deal more of the prosperity consciousness than I did. I was raised the son of a farmer and rancher, and I had nothing. My father came from a Canadian ranch, in fact, and had his own goodly ranch. He sold the ranch to his father for a dollar.

Then he went to the United States, thinking that he would receive the ranch back when his father died. But his younger brother stayed at home and worked the ranch and wormed his way, into his father's heart. So his father left the ranch to the younger brother and my father was defrauded of it.

My father didn't have too many skills. He was not well educated, and he had to work hard for his money. He could have done well on the big Canadian ranch, but in the States he had a pretty tough time of it. He passed away when I was nine years old. My mother was not strong, and she was very upset and nervous because she had to support a nine-year-old child on her own. Many times I didn't have anything in the house to eat except maybe two or three slices of bread.

So when I went into the United States Air Force in World War II, my mother was a widow living alone in a small home and she had little money. I gave her an army allotment check of about twenty-five dollars, and she was able to earn about twenty-five dollars a month. So she had about fifty dollars a month to live on, which wasn't much for food, bus fare, taxes, upkeep on a house and a few other things. It was pretty rough. So when I came out of the army I had nothing.

Elizabeth was a little different. She didn't have anything either. But she became a Christian Scientist when she was nine years old and she learned their concepts of prosperity. I was trained more along the Methodist church lines. In fact, I was a member of the same church as the former Senator Alexander Wiley.

Senator Wiley was one of the wealthy people in my hometown. There were a lot of wealthy people who were Methodists and a few of us poor people who were Methodists. We all sat alongside of each other in church, but that was about the extent of our contact.

So there was a great deal of difference between my consciousness of prosperity and Elizabeth's. When I started out in this work, I was a little afraid. I know what it means to wonder where your next meal or your next dollar is coming from. Elizabeth didn't have any of this. She was trained practically from childhood to think in terms of God supplying her needs.

I received a great deal of my education on prosperity from Elizabeth. She used to say to me, "Well, now God wants us to have that, so we're going to put a down payment on it." I'd say, "Well, we haven't got enough money to pay for it.

What's the matter with you? We can't do that." She would say, "God can supply all of our needs. Now, we're just going to put a down payment on it, and if we can't pay for it, we'll just forget about it."

That woman has changed my whole way of thinking since I've known her. I wouldn't be at all surprised that if she went over to London and saw London Bridge and decided to buy it, she would come up with the money. She would put a down payment on it and probably wind up owning it. I'm sure she would convince the British crown to give up London Bridge!

So a great deal of what I have learned about prosperity has been the result of the masters working with Elizabeth. I'm sure you realize that

I had something to give her in return, because there were other things that were given to me. I was one of those of whom it is said, "Blessed are the poor in spirit, for theirs is the kingdom of heaven."

The two of us together have been able to find out a great deal about the secrets of prosperity because we give our prosperity to The Summit Lighthouse, and this is good.

TENTH SECRET

ALWAYS KEEP A SEED OF PROSPERITY AND KEEP YOUR THOUGHTS UPLIFTED

Some of you don't realize that when we started this activity, I wore suits from the Heck Company, by heck, in Washington, D.C. These suits with two pairs of pants cost nineteen dollars. I remember standing on the stage in this absolutely grand home in front of this woman worth sixteen million dollars with this baggy suit on worth nineteen dollars. She sat right there in her royal robes and never shelled out anything to take care of that problem. For almost a year I wore that kind of equipment.

But then the masters explained the laws of prosperity to me and I started using these laws. The first thing you know, I began sporting tailor-made suits.

So we have learned about prosperity the hard way, and we know that these laws work for everybody. There isn't anyone who has to be without anything he needs, and there's no reason to have more than you really need.

Some people say, "Well, I'm going to put some money away for a rainy day." I think it's a good idea to be prudent.

Master Morya taught me this several years ago when I was in rather strait circumstances. Once after I had paid a bill, I had six dollars left in my pocket and a mountain of debts. I was driving a brand-new Lincoln. I didn't even have the money to telegraph a friend of mine who was a millionaire and who would have loaned me some money.

So Master Morya came along and said, "Now, enough of this foolishness." I said, "What do you mean?" He said, "What you have to remember is that no matter how poor you are, always keep one hundred dollars somewhere that you can fall back on. You don't have to keep a lot, but always keep at least one hundred dollars in cash tucked away somewhere."

I know that very few of you are what you would call poor. It doesn't matter. It's still a mighty good idea to always have at least one hundred dollars in either cash or traveler's checks on your person or concealed somewhere.

This is good advice for anyone. I'm going to tell you why. Master Morya showed me that this is seed for prosperity.

When you're down to your last penny—and it's a terrible feeling when you're down to your last penny—you don't have anything at all to fall back on except maybe your friends. You go to your friends and sure as shootin' they'll tell you that they couldn't possibly help you because all kinds of things have happened, or all their money is in bonds.

So keep a seed of prosperity and keep your thoughts very, very much in an uplifted state. Now, this is hard to do when you are down and out. If it weren't hard to do, more people would do it.

If you will learn to not let go of every cent but to hang on to enough to tide you over in case you get into trouble, you will have confidence in that seed. Then you can apply to God and he will provide you with the wisdom to know how to use what you have in order to get more. But if you use everything up until you're broke and bent and twisted and turned, then your confidence will often be shaken.

I think that the Lord put me through that once to teach me the law. I had to experience this so I would know how to advise other people, because all kinds of people come to us in this activity—from paupers to millionaires, from farmers to industrialists.

We have among our members some very splendid people. Sometimes the man with a million dollars may ask your advice just as much as the man with nothing, and we want to be able to advise people correctly.

PRIME THE PUMP

*Y*our thoughts have a great deal to do with your prosperity, and sometimes the way to break a pattern is to spend money. There have been times when everything was going badly and I went out and bought an expensive suit—right in the midst of the worst downfall. I got such a lift from wearing that suit that my whole mind went up. And the first thing you know, the money was flowing again.

It's the old pump-priming situation. You have to release something from yourself because you're suffering from mental stagnation. That's the whole secret of prosperity.

As I said, the reason prosperity doesn't flow into people's worlds is because they have stopped giving. It doesn't matter how much water is in a pipe. You can have just a trickle of water, but if there is nothing to stop it, you can get that water to flow.

That's why pump priming is valuable. That's why a woman can go out and buy a new dress. She can get herself an expensive jewel sometimes. The lift from that and the release of the money will start the supply coming again.

You have to understand how to work with the laws of abundance. You not only work with them through prayer and right thinking, but also by seeing that the law of stagnation does not function in your world to dam up your supply.

This is why some of the great multi-millionaires have taken tremendous risks and they have sometimes come out right on top. It's not a matter of luck. It's a matter of using the law.

TWELFTH SECRET

UNDERSTAND THAT PROSPERITY IS AN ACTIVITY OF THE SPIRIT

I'm always concerned that people understand that prosperity is more an activity of the Spirit than of the flesh. A lot of us like to think that prosperity is something that is of the flesh—that if we use the laws, then a great deal of money is released into our world.

Money is what people always seem to want. But that's not really the answer. Happiness, contentment, peace of mind, understanding, compassion, tolerance and every good quality of life are worth more than anything else. Money cannot buy these.

Yet you can't live in the modern world without money, unless you're a peace pilgrim or somebody like that. You can use the begging bowl, as the poor do in India. They run around with a begging bowl, and all day long they beg until somebody has pity on them and drops a coin in their cup and they go out and buy their meal.

I don't think most of us could live that way, particularly if we have families. I know The Summit Lighthouse couldn't live that way because we have a printing press to maintain so we can keep on publishing the teachings of the great masters.

THIRTEENTH SECRET

WHEN YOU ARE TEMPTED TO WORRY, TURN YOUR THOUGHTS TO GOD

---

*I*t's interesting how God has provided for our needs. I think that every one of you should develop faith that God will take care of your needs no matter what they are. Nobody in the world should worry about their future. In fact, that's one way of damming up the flow of goods into your world.

Worry will definitely cut you off.

The minute you start worrying, you tune in to millions of other people who are worrying. You won't know it, but their thoughts will be attracted like a magnet into your subconscious and your world. And the first thing you know, you'll be going down, down, down, down because of their thoughts.

Among the greatest secrets of prosperity is to tune into right thinking by thinking right yourself. Turn your thoughts to God and the masters and to an inexhaustible sense of supply. Learn to develop the feeling that "no matter what I need, it will be supplied to me."

A lot of people laugh at me because of what I said to the man from whom we bought our last house. Down below the hill there was a concrete pad, and I said,

"That's our landing port for our helicopter."

Well, a helicopter's worth many thousands of dollars. I had the idea that God would provide me with a helicopter and I'd learn how to fly it and I'd be able to fly around the United States and give lectures.

We don't have it yet, but the house cost a lot more money than a helicopter and the Lord provided for the house. We still think that when we get a ranch and we get our university we'll have a helicopter to fly over here to this area. Maybe we can travel all around the country in it.

Elizabeth says she won't fly with me. Her consciousness of prosperity is very great, but she doesn't seem to have faith in my perspicacity in flying a helicopter!

I hope that I've helped you a little with this talk. I could have made it longer, but I felt that the points that I gave would be of value. You can always fill the cup so full that it's running over, but I hope I've put at least a half a cup of goodies into this talk for you.

KEYS TO CREATIVE ABUNDANCE

1. Be grateful for everything that happens to you.

2. Forgive yourself.

3. Abandon anxiety.

4. Fire up your faith.

5. Visualize your dreams coming true.

6. Practice the science of the immaculate concept.

7. Clear your subconscious.

8. Make a treasure map.

9. Follow the nine steps to precipitation.

10. Meditate on the creation of the cloud of infinite energy.

SECRETS OF PROSPERITY

1. Never dam up the flow of your energy.

2. Give ten percent of yourself to God.

3. Give in secret.

4. Give something, no matter how small.

5. Use the gifts God has given you.

6. Think of the world as your family.

7. Remember that the God Presence is the source of your supply.

8. Call upon Fortuna.

9. Depend on God.

10. Always keep a seed of prosperity and keep your thoughts uplifted.

11. Prime the pump.

12. Understand that prosperity is an activity of the Spirit.

13. When you are tempted to worry, turn your thoughts to God.

NOTES

Abandon Anxiety
1. For more information about the violet flame, see Elizabeth Clare Prophet, *Violet Flame to Heal Body, Mind and Soul* (Corwin Springs, Mont.: Summit University Press, 1997).

The Art of Treasure Mapping
1. The Summit Lighthouse was founded in 1958 by Mark L. Prophet to publish the teachings of the ascended masters, the saints and sages of East and West who have attained union with God.

The teachings of Saint Germain quoted in this book, including "Nine Steps to Precipitation" and "Meditation on the Creation of the Cloud," are taken from *Saint Germain On Alchemy: Formulas for Self-Transformation* (Livingston, Mont.: Summit University Press, 1993).

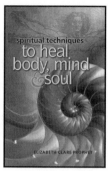

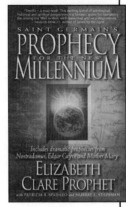

SUMMIT UNIVERSITY 🔥 PRESS®

POCKET GUIDES TO
PRACTICAL SPIRITUALITY SERIES

Karma and Reincarnation
Transcending Your Past, Transforming Your Future

Alchemy of the Heart:
How to Give and Receive More Love

Your Seven Energy Centers:
*A Holistic Approach to Physical,
Emotional and Spiritual Vitality*

The Art of Practical Spirituality:
*How to Bring More Passion, Creativity
and Balance into Everyday Life*

Soul Mates and Twin Flames:
The Spiritual Dimension of Love and Relationships

How to Work with Angels

Access the Power of Your Higher Self:
*Your Source of Inner Guidance
and Spiritual Transformation*

The Creative Power of Sound:
Affirmations to Create, Heal and Transform

Creative Abundance:
Keys to Spiritual and Material Prosperity

Violet Flame to Heal Body, Mind and Soul

Summit University Press books are available from fine
bookstores everywhere. For a free catalog or to place
an order, please call 1-800-245-5445 or 406-848-9500.